The abuse of drugs

A Christian View

David Pott
Duncan Vere

Inter-Varsity Press

Universities & Colleges Christian Fellowship
39 Bedford Square, London WC1B 3EY

First published March 1975

ISBN 0 85110 228 X

Printed in Great Britain by G. P. Printers, Devon

Contents

Publisher's Preface

The two chapters comprising this small book were written independently but complement each other in a most helpful way.

David Pott, who has had considerable experience of work among drug users, looks at the causes underlying the drug problem and provides factual information about the drugs chiefly involved and the extent of the abuse.

Professor Vere, who is Head of the Department of Pharmacology and Therapeutics, London Hospital Medical College, is interested in drug dependence not only as a pharmacological problem but also through his work with alcoholic men in the Salvation Army Hostel in Whitechapel. He therefore looks at the problem in a wider context. Why do people become dependent on drugs and other substances? What sort of people are they? He then provides what he calls a 'spiritual analysis'. In four brief studies he looks at passages from the New Testament which, he believes, throw light on what he calls 'distorted dependence'. Questions are provided to point up the relevance of the passages chosen to the discussion. These can be used either for independent study or for group discussion.

It is not sufficient for Christians to understand the problem more clearly. They will want to do something about it. How can the drug user be helped? Both authors conclude their papers with practical suggestions as well as some warnings.

1 A Christian view of the drug scene

David Pott

THE BACKGROUND TO THE PROBLEM

The growth of a serious drug problem in the western world is not an accidental phenomenon. The rise in the incidence of alcoholism, the use of syringes, and the existence of the pro-pot brigade are all logical outcomes of the kind of society we live in today. New ideas about life and its meaning are exerting an increasing influence. Drugs abuse is just one symptom of a *malaise* which has its roots in these changes in man's way of thinking. Many, for example, have abandoned that concept of truth which acknowledged the reality of God and the devil, of heaven and hell, of right and wrong, of thesis and antithesis. The philosophies of secularism, relativism and synthesis, which were once the preserve of a few intellectuals, have filtered down after many years into the general culture. This jettisoning of the traditional Christian framework leads to difficulties in the areas of reality, the nature of man and the nature of morality, all of which have consequences in the field of drug abuse. Let us examine each of these three factors in turn.

a. The nature of reality

Most older people find it hard to understand young people asking such questions as, 'How do I know what is real?' This is because they have accepted (subconsciously perhaps) that God created the real external world. The present generation, however, has no valid concept of reality. When a thoughtful teenager looks at a daffodil he may say to himself, 'Perhaps, if I take

LSD, I may be able to appreciate the beauty of the daffodil more fully.' LSD helps to push a person who is insecure about reality to the logical but desperate conclusion of his position. So the Beatles in their LSD phase could sing 'Nothing is real', and others can lose their grasp of reality to such an extent that they think they can fly.

It is misleading to suppose that only the more intelligent user of hallucinogenic drugs has this particular problem. The person who blots out his past with barbiturates or 'drowns his sorrows' in alcohol also has a deficient view of reality. It is commonly held that drug users are attempting to escape from reality, but the truth is that they have never known reality in a comprehensive way. This is well demonstrated by the fact that in their more sober moments they will describe life as being like 'a nightmare' or 'a bad trip'. Those who have been brought up in an unreal and artificial environment, such as the tenement blocks of Harlem or high-rise flats in London, are particularly susceptible to drug-taking. There is a close link between pollution and the misuse of drugs. The person who sees only ugly sights and hears only the noise of a city's traffic is likely to be attracted by the promise of LSD to produce colourful visual and auditory experiences.

b. The nature of man

'How do I know I have significance ?' is again a question which many are asking today. Clearly they are facing an identity crisis. Experts give differing answers to the problem of the nature of man. They include the view that he is a 'naked ape', or that he is totally determined by genetical, environmental and social factors, as the behaviourists would claim. This type of view reduces man to a machine, and in a highly technological society more and more people are vulnerable to this sort of pressure to see themselves as a small cog in a vast machine. Machines can be 'turned on' or 'plugged in', they 'buzz' and they 'flash'. Surely there is some significance in the fact that drug terminology employs these machine-like terms? By using such terms, the drug user shows that he has a low view of human worth. Low self-esteem is also a predisposing factor for the alcoholic or heroin addict.

It is well known that addicts often share syringes and some have even used toilet water for fixing. They are usually aware of the extreme danger of such practices but have such a poor self-concept that they feel their identities are not worth preserving. The formation of identity depends very much on models, and in particular on the models of one's parents. Obviously the person with inadequate parents starts with a tremendous handicap in the formation of his identity, and he tends to look around for other models in a rather undiscriminating way, often with unfortunate consequences. Christians, of course, have a unique 'model' in the person of Jesus Christ, and it is also valid for them to model on other Christians who demonstrate clearly the character of Jesus (see Philippians 3 : 17).

c. The nature of the moral order

Then again, fewer people today believe in an objective moral order in which what is 'right' and what is 'wrong' can be clearly identified. If there is no objective moral order, it is much easier, of course, to justify personal action. It does not matter if one transgresses traditional morality. Ours is the day of 'do your *own* thing'. The current stress on subjectivism means that there is a strong pressure on people to have 'experiences'. The trend is to internalize – to find answers inside yourself. Some of the sections in Timothy Leary's *Politics of Ecstasy* are headed 'Start your *own* religion', and

'Write your *own* Bible'. The person with a subjective philosophy, who has no belief in objective morality, is on very shaky ground if he condemns drug use. As Christians, we know that there is a real, objective moral order, based on the unchanging character of God himself. The existence of this moral order is what causes real guilt in thousands of people. (This guilt would be dismissed as guilt-feelings by those who do not believe in objective morality.) Sedation through alcohol, barbiturates or opiates seems an excellent way to obliterate a torturing sense of guilt.

It is hardly surprising, therefore, that the philosophy of many people today encourages the use of drugs. Furthermore, we live in a highly technological society which is dominated by the competitive spirit and commercial exploitation. The alcohol, tobacco and pharmaceutical industries use high-pressure salesmanship to keep their sales high. Doctors are under pressure to use new drugs as they come on the market, and the sheer weight of numbers of patients means that a high amount of prescription is inevitable. LSD and cannabis are also advertised, but in a slightly different way, as part of the counter-culture. This counter-culture (also called the 'Underground' or 'alternative society') includes a few people who are excellent in the field of media communications. The underground papers and magazines, rock festivals and records, and books such as *Bomb Culture* by Jeff Nuttall, *Play Power* by Richard Neville and *The Politics of Ecstasy* by Timothy Leary are all promoting the counter-culture, and doing it very well. To the average sixth-former, an hour reading *Play Power* would make a much greater impact than an hour listening to the local policeman or a GP warning against the dangers of drugs.

TYPES OF DRUGS

Having seen that the existence of drug use of all kinds is not surprising, we shall now consider the different kinds of drugs that are abused today.

a. The opiates

When the average man in the street thinks of a drug addict, he envisages someone plunging a needle into his arm and injecting heroin. Yet the number of 'pure' opiate addicts in this country is very small. In practice addicts do not stick to one drug of addiction such as heroin, but switch from one to another according to availability. The phenomenon of the poly-drug user has become far more common in recent years. In December 1972, 1,619 individuals in the United Kingdom were receiving supplies of opiates, but this figure bears little or no relation to the number of injecting addicts. Most drug clinics supply a heroin-substitute, methadone, to addicts. Because some addicts do not like methadone, they obtain their drugs elsewhere, and are consequently not on the 'official' lists. Also a number of those receiving methadone at the clinics sell it on the black market, and then obtain other drugs with their profits. I know five addicts in Sheffield who have been on a prescription for methadone, but at least thirty people who are seriously addicted.

The opiates are, as the word suggests, derivatives of opium, but cocaine too is usually included in this group, although its stimulant action is the exact reverse of the sedating effect of heroin and morphine.

In order to obtain the desired effects of the drug, the addict has gradually to increase his dosage, and his body accustoms to a dose which would kill a normal person. This is known as tolerance. Deaths sometimes occur from an overdose after a period in prison or hospital, when the addict has failed to allow for the decrease in tolerance caused by his abstinence. Other causes of death include deliberate suicide, death by septicaemia due to the introduction of infection through using dirty needles, and poisoning through impure substances. Some time ago in London a girl died after being sold the detergent Ajax instead of heroin.

b. Sedatives

There is a vast array of sedatives available today, ranging from dangerous substances such as phenobarbitone or mandrax, to a relatively mild hypnotic such as librium. Ironically, a very serious barbiturate addiction problem grew during the fifties and sixties, and all the while the media were concentrating on the few young people abusing the opiates. A large proportion of barbiturate addicts are aged between forty and sixty, and many go undetected. In his book *The Drugtakers*, Jock Young, extrapolating from T. H. Bewley's figures, estimates that there are between 75,000 and 125,000 dependent barbiturate users in the United Kingdom, and a further 400,000 to 600,000 who are regular but not dependent users. There is growing evidence that this acceptance of usually legal drug use in parents means that their children will be more willing to use *illegal* drug substances.

Drug users are more violent and manipulative when on barbiturates than on any other drug. Moreover, the barbiturates are often taken with alcohol, which accentuates the problems still further. I personally am relieved when, instead of barbiturates, opiates such as heroin or diconal are available on the market, because people are much more placid on the opiates. Barbiturates are generally taken orally, but a proportion of younger users inject them. Some users take the barbiturates reluctantly. They know the damage that is being done to them, and if opiates were available and cheaper, they would use them instead. Unfortunately barbiturates are very cheap – a capsule of tuinal costs only 20p here in Sheffield, while methadone is £1.50 an ampoule.

The easy availability of barbiturates is alarming, and is well demonstrated by a campaign in Sheffield called DUMP (Disposal of Unwanted Medicines and Poisons) held from 1 to 15 October 1973. This was a scheme whereby people were asked to hand in tablets voluntarily to chemists. The estimated total recovery was 589,760. This included 19,700 barbiturates. Although the campaign was well advertised, it is likely that these figures represent only a fraction of what is left around in Sheffield homes.

c. Amphetamines

Amphetamines have a stimulant effect on the central nervous system, hence the slang term 'speed'. Again there is in this group a wide variety of drugs, the most dangerous of which is methylamphetamine or methedrine. Like the barbiturates, they are sometimes injected. A heavy user of amphetamines often reaches a crisis-point where he hasn't been sleeping for days, as his mind is being kept awake, but his body is craving for sleep. This leads to a point where the person 'crashes-out' into unconsciousness. Other users take 'sleepers' (barbiturates) to induce the much needed sleep, and thus get caught in a vicious circle.

d. Hallucinogens

Strictly speaking these drugs cause illusions rather than hallucinations. They include peyote, mescaline, DMT and STP, but by far the commonest in this country is lysergide or LSD ('acid'). LSD is extremely difficult to detect. There is no smell, and the average dose is only 100 microgrammes. In recent years there has been a rapid rise in the number of arrests in Great Britain for possession of LSD. There were only 166 arrests in 1969, but in 1970 there were 744 and in 1971, 1,537. LSD is not addictive, and many trip just a few times and then give it up. This is not to say that it is relatively harmless. The effects of LSD are extremely unpredictable. The number of accidental deaths due to taking it is very hard to estimate because of the difficulties of detection, but the fact is well known that a user's view of reality is grossly distorted. All too often terms such as 'mind-expansion', or increased 'awareness', are euphemisms for sense-distortion. The user has no yardstick to assess reality, and is at the mercy of his own subjective impressions.

LSD is a drug of optimism, which was the prevailing mood of the hippy culture, as opposed to the gloomy pessimism of the beats (called 'beatniks' by the media). But this optimism was blind and shallow. All the flower-power and the smiles were a cover-up for futility and despair. This is why some people, after a 'freaking-out' stage using LSD, suddenly turned to heroin, the drug of despair. There is no close pharmacological connection between these drugs, and the cause was obviously philosophic. They realized the superficiality of their optimism, and suddenly plunged into despair.

e. Cannabis

There are an estimated 200 million cannabis smokers in the world. In Great Britain there must be at least a million who have tried the drug at some time or other, and in some groups it has replaced alcohol and is viewed as a mild social relaxant. There is a wide difference in potency, ranging from the more powerful cannabis resin (hashish) to the leaves and flowers of cannabis (marijuana or 'grass'). Some of the underground papers advertise several different brands of cannabis. The initial effect of cannabis is a stimulating one, but its over-all effect is one of sedation. Sense-distortion also takes place, though not on the same scale as with LSD.

There have been no known deaths as a result of smoking cannabis, but when cannabis resin is taken with tobacco, the health risks inherent in tobacco will of course apply. The damage that cannabis causes in the physical realm is related to the THC (tetrahydrocannabinol) content. THC, unlike such substances as alcohol and LSD, does not pass through the body quickly, but takes about seven to ten days to do so. The occasional smoker is therefore doing himself no great physical damage. But the regular smoker is building up the THC content in the body fats. This slows a person down, and lethargy is a well-known effect of cannabis.

Most research into cannabis tends to concentrate on the physical effects of the drug and, as such, is rather limited, because drug use is obviously bound up very much with a person's total viewpoint and lifestyle. The effects of cannabis tend to strengthen and reinforce a particular set of views, which before smoking may have been rather tenuously held. So, for example, a person may be confirmed in his view that society is repressive when he is hounded by the authorities as a suspected pot-smoker.

f. Alcohol

Recent research in Manchester suggests that the conventional estimate of between 200,000 and 400,000[1] alcoholics in Great Britain is far too low. It was discovered that some doctors had as many as thirty or more alcoholics among their patients rather than the three or four suggested by the conventional figures. Suffice it to say that alcoholism is a very serious

[1] Figures from *Alcohol Abuse* (Office of Health Economics, London, 1970).

problem in the western world. In Great Britain the half million or more alcoholics affect in their turn many relatives and associates. A significant number of young people are becoming alcoholics. Also, a large number of people who are not alcoholics, but who have had a 'few too many', are involved in car accidents that end in fatalities. The suicide rate among alcoholics is eighty times the national average. Crude spirit drinking including the use of methylated spirits and surgical spirits is the worst form of addiction, and usually kills a person in about three years. This compares with the thirty years a heavy brandy drinker would probably live. In 1972 people in the United Kingdom spent £2,948 million on alcoholic beverages.[2] While statistics do not tell us the whole story, they indicate that this is a really desperate problem compared with, say, that of the opiates.

g. Tobacco

Thousands of people who talk disparagingly of 'drug addicts' are in fact addicts themselves. Nicotine is a highly addictive drug, and anyone smoking more than about thirty cigarettes a day is well 'hooked'. They need to smoke a cigarette about once every half-hour to maintain the maximum effect on the brain. The difficulties of giving up cigarette smoking are well illustrated by the low success rate of smoking clinics, which is between 12% and 20% after one year. Those who have been through withdrawal from opiates sometimes find it an even greater struggle to give up smoking cigarettes. Between 50,000 and 80,000 people die each year from causes directly attributable to cigarette smoking. It is interesting to note that, because doctors are especially aware of the health risks involved, many of them have given up smoking.

[2] Quoted from *Social Trends* (HMSO, 1972).

This has resulted in a marked drop in the death rate from lung cancer among that profession.

The British Government is in a difficult situation regarding tobacco, as it receives about £3 million per day (that is, 20% of its revenue) from cigarette consumption. This makes the £100,000 a year spent on anti-smoking propaganda seem rather absurd. The tobacco industries themselves spend £50 million a year advertising cigarettes.

HELPING THE DRUG USER

In this section I shall concern myself with the younger user of illegal substances, although some of this will be relevant to other drug users.

Since the middle sixties, the drug scene has held a peculiar fascination for Christians. This fascination has been distinctly unhealthy and has hindered a genuine Christian approach in helping drug users. It probably sprang up partly because the converted drug addict was seen as a more glorious 'trophy of God's grace' than the converted housewife next door. Some Christians rushed rather hastily in search of drug addicts after reading such books as *The Cross and the Switchblade*, feeling that the effect on them of such books constituted 'a call'. The West End junkies, however, are fairly perceptive, and they quickly spotted those situations where 'conversion' was the necessary pre-condition for food and other material help. I have met several addicts who have simulated conversion in order to obtain help from gullible Christians.

Some more problems emerged when the use of drug terminology to convey the gospel became popular. In the first place, there were few who could use the jargon naturally, so this led to some well-deserved ridicule and ah carge of falseness. Secondly, some on the drug scene, when urged to 'turn on to Jesus', accepted a Jesus experience totally in the terms of their past drug experiences. When the 'high' faded away they felt disillusioned, and became less open to the gospel. Thirdly, this approach made the gospel seem just another answer, and not in any sense the basic truth about God, life and man. The drug scene is intensely relativistic and Christians engaging in an experience contest do not help in this respect at all. There are several cults appealing to folk in the drug scene on the platform of better experiences, and it is useless to appeal exclusively on this level, as if the 'Jesus trip' were just another good buy on the spiritual supermarket.

How, then, can the Christian help the drug user in a genuine way? The following points are not, of course, complete, but they are offered as a basis for further thought and action.

a. Responsibility

A popular understanding of drug misuse is that the addict is the unfortunate victim of circumstances such as the broken home, bad social environment or meeting up with an evil drug pusher. Similarly, some experts would claim that addicts are suffering from some form of mental illness such as psychopathy or schizophrenia. Those who totally accept these 'unfortunate victim' theories are unable to relate to addicts as true human beings. They were just programmed the wrong way.

As Christians we would not deny the significance of these tragic background factors, but they must never be allowed to disguise the reality of personal responsibility. Resorting to drug abuse is a wrong response to a bad situation. This may seem a banal thing to say, and we should acknowledge heartily that we would probably have responded no better in similar circumstances; but still the fact of responsibility remains. We must realize the addict's responsibility in order to relate to him as a *person*, and it is equally necessary for the addict to realize this in order that he can become a *whole* person again. Accepting responsibility is often the first step in the right direction.

b. Presuppositions

In the same way that Paul and other early Christians were at pains to understand the thought-pattern of the people to whom they took the gospel, we should be concerned to understand the thinking of the drug scene. All too often people think they can learn about the drug scene by reading about drugs and their effects. But it is no use knowing about pharmacology unless you also understand something of the addict's cultural milieu. For example, it is futile to attempt to 'cure an addict' if he feels there is 'no life before death'. His drug use is consistent with his despair. Again it is useless to talk about the effects of cannabis to a person who believes, as Richard Neville does, that 'laziness is a good thing'. What is needed in these kinds of situation is a different viewpoint to start with. By their using the drug, most LSD users are being consistent with their philosophic viewpoint. These presuppositions suggest that 'the ultimate' is beyond understanding, and therefore the person must 'blow the mind' to get through to that ultimate reality. Until he sees anything wrong with this basic premise his LSD use is quite logical.

Before Jesus revealed himself to the woman at the well, he very gently, but firmly, showed her the falseness of her life-style. In the same way, the Christian's life-style and his thinking should challenge the assumptions of the person who uses drugs. It seems to me that some drug addicts have been hustled into premature 'spiritual births', and consequently they fall back into drugs again. They have not fully understood the corruption of their former life-style, and have therefore not experienced a real repentance, which, after all, means basically a proper turning away from the past.

c. Coping with the whole person

With a problem like the misuse of drugs it is very tempting to treat the person as three separate parts rather than a whole. For example, I can think of one person in prison who was seen by a doctor when he had withdrawal symptoms on arrival, by a psychiatrist because he was feeling paranoid, and by the prison chaplain when he attempted suicide. All these three had legitimate functions in relation to the body, mind and spirit, but the great need for that man was to find someone to relate to him as a *whole* person. I cannot think of any person who has broken free from a severe drug problem without having a meaningful relationship with someone.

In Amos chapter 8 there is a passage which speaks with great relevance to the situation of the post-war generation in the West today: '"Behold, the days are coming," says the Lord God, "when I will send a famine on the land; not a famine of bread, nor a thirst for water, but of hearing the words of the Lord. They shall wander from sea to sea, and from north to east; they shall run to and fro, to seek the word of the Lord, but they shall not find it. In that day the fair virgins and the young men shall faint for thirst."' Young people in our affluent society are not aware of material shortages, but there is a great famine of meaning and purpose. This causes an aimless wandering (sometimes towards the East!), but all ends in futility. The exhaustion and apathy of the whole personality is well expressed in verse 13. The same thought occurs in Isaiah 40 : 30, but verse 31 goes on to speak of those who 'wait for the Lord' and who gain wholeness of body, mind and spirit.

The gospel is for the whole man, and the deepest and most meaningful relationship a person can have is one with God himself, through Jesus Christ. Although I have warned against a Christian approach which majors on 'experience', it is important to stress that I do believe we need to include this aspect as we present the gospel. A genuine experience of God (as opposed to an irrational, unverifiable 'trip') is offered to those who respond to the truth.

d. Forgiveness

As we have already seen, drugs, and especially alcohol, the opiates and the sedatives, are used to cover up guilt. Addicts feel guilt about their addiction, about people they have let down and about the things they have done to get drugs. I know a girl who gave heroin to someone, who overdosed on it and died. She sought advice from many people about her acute guilt problem, but none could help until she heard about the work of Jesus on the cross. The assurance of God's forgiveness was an overwhelming benefit to her. It did not mean that she became carefree about what she had done, but at least the guilt and the despair were gone.

e. Power

It is difficult for those of us who have never become dependent on alcohol or other drugs to realize the power of their hold over people. Occasionally, too, there are additional complications when people have opened themselves to Satan by dabbling in the occult.[3]

John writes that 'The reason the Son of God appeared was to destroy the works of the devil' (1 John 3 : 8), and Christ's redemptive work means that the power

[3] I do not subscribe to the view that all addicts are demon-possessed, although such addiction is a manifestation of the devil's general power in the world (1 John 5 : 19). I am convinced, however, that this occurs in specific cases, usually when the person has opened himself to it. Note, therefore, that he is *still* responsible.

of the Holy Spirit can rescue and guard a person from the power of addiction. God is sovereign and sometimes he chooses to deliver a person instantaneously from the desire to take drugs. But sometimes he chooses to allow a person to prove God's grace and power day by day by resisting the temptation which may remain indefinitely. The latter instance is just as great a witness to God's power as is the former.

The true objective of anyone involved in helping a drug user should be to encourage that person to conform not so much to normal society as to the truth. The drug user has a faulty view of the structure of reality: he may believe that there are no real structures, that reality is strictly limited to his own unpleasant experiences in life, or that spiritual truth is beyond understanding. It is exciting to observe someone, who has had such a faulty view, gradually finding the structures of reality. As Jesus said, 'the truth will make you free'. When a person discovers that the external world is real, that he is a person of value, that there are objective guide-lines for behaviour, and that there really is a personal God, his viewpoint is altered, and drug use becomes illogical and unnecessary. This is no easy thing, and many people prefer their fake view of reality, which may, for example, allow them to avoid personal responsibility.

In conclusion, then, we must avoid thinking narrowly about drugs. It is an issue which throws us back to questions about the deeper meaning of life, and about the total cultural situation we face in the closing third of this century. 'Where there is no vision (a clear grasp of reality), the people perish.'

2 The problem of distorted dependence

Duncan Vere

INTRODUCTION

Everyone who studies people must have been struck by the fact that many gain immense satisfaction, often it seems an abnormal satisfaction, from certain things which the majority enjoy to some extent. They are overtaken by an exaggeration of one or more of the pleasures of what is regarded as 'normal' living. It may be religious observances (as opposed to faith), or it may be food. It may be money, or alchohol, or tobacco, It may be a house, or a drug. It may be social esteem. or physical prowess. It may be sexual performance, or gambling, or taking risks. Most people would say that they need, or can enjoy in some measure, all or most of these things. But some become 'fixed' on one or more of them, so that their life increasingly finds its focus in them, and their attention is more and more preoccupied with acquiring them. They come to depend on them, not in any normal, healthy way, but in a stronger fashion which begins to control them, determining what they do, moulding their character and activity. Eventually they come to feel that they are not living unless they can acquire or hold on to their own particular 'prop'. This is 'distorted dependence'.

I should make clear at once that I am not attempting to make some slick and superficial theory cover all these problems; nor am I trying to assert that there is just one common mechanism which underlies them.[1]

[1] W. D. M. Paton (*World Medicine*, 22 May 1974, p. 31) has drawn together, however, impressive evidence that a common *epidemiological* pattern may underlie dependence upon substances as diverse as alcohol, heroin and cannabis.

Not so. There are, for example, well-known pharmacological differences which largely determine which drugs will be involved in patterns of distorted dependence and which will not. There are strong 'drugs of dependence', such as diamorphine (heroin) and morphine, and drugs which go with weaker dependence patterns, such as cannabis, coffee and aspirin. Personality factors also matter. There are some people to whom alcohol quickly becomes a serious menace; others follow a pattern of moderate drinking for many years, though a change in their circumstances can sometimes transform them into alcohol-dependents. The same is true of food and tobacco. There are also social factors. In the London Hospital everyone is today given tea and no-one receives gin. Soon after the Hospital was founded in the mid-eighteenth century the converse was the rule, largely for fiscal reasons. Gin-dependence was rife in East London in the century which followed. Tea-dependence is now scarcely a problem!

Among the many factors, then, which are associated with human misery (and they are many) distorted dependence can frequently be seen. Sometimes it turns up as a surprise. Dependence upon religious observance, for example, may mimic holiness until it is seen to be what it really is, a thing which can cramp and distort life, turning it into a form of slavery far removed from God's revealed objectives for mankind.

There was a time when all forms of dependence were scorned as weaknesses, and the ideal of a strong, independent man was valued. Since the few people who managed to achieve independence were often selfish isolates, the idea of independence has been replaced in modern education by interdependence – each supplying what he can for the needs of others. Not all, however, would support this excellent (and biblical) idea. 'What is wrong with being dependent', they ask, 'if, as a result, life is more satisfactory than it would otherwise have been? Why shouldn't somebody "get hooked" by a habit, pleasure or satisfaction, provided no-one else gets harmed? It is his own business what he does, and he knows best what suits his own personality.'

Two things seem wrong with that idea. First of all, most people, whether they accept a Christian viewpoint or not, would agree that distorted dependence damages. It can narrow the personality, shutting it up to a mere habit which pre-empts attention, resources, learning and emotional life. It can enslave. It can often destroy people mentally or physically. The alcoholic with liver disease, the smoker with lung cancer, the religious ascetic who starves, are all examples of those who have not lived to the full. It is estimated that somewhere between 300,000 and half a million people are dependent upon alcohol in Britain now, to the point of being unable to manage their own lives fully. No-one should minimize the damage done from this cause alone in the lives of such people and those close to them. True, some forms of dependence are less costly. Take, for example, the large numbers of unhappy, middle-aged women who take sleeping-pills and tranquillizers too frequently. But even that is an enormous expense to them or to the National Health Service and involves their doctors in a morass of unnecessary medication.

The second reason is more important, once it is accepted. It is that Christ, and his apostles, taught that a man is not his own, to please himself about what he may do with his body, his mind or his possessions. If that is understood and accepted, the problem of distorted dependence takes on a new, and obviously spiritual, dimension. The reasons given for this seemingly outrageous intervention in a man's privacy are first that God made him,[2] and second that, through

[2] Psalm 24: 1-5.

the death of Christ, God has bought him.[3] So a man can gain only an illusory independence by frank rebellion. Seen in this light, God's intervention is not an outrage, it is his logical right and prerogative.

Whether one accepts either argument, both, or neither, there is more to be considered about distorted dependence, simply because it is so great a problem.

WHO ARE THE CASUALTIES?

The casualties are ordinary people, like you and me. In the case of drug dependence, exhaustive enquiries have revealed no personality pattern which is characteristically susceptible,[4] except that they can be summed up as 'inadequate'. But who is adequate? It is not an all-or-nothing quality. There are grades of inadequacy in us all, and whether or not we prove adequate is relative to what happens round about us. For example, many officers with distinguished war records take to drink because they cannot face the inaction of peace. They may be very adequate in some spheres, but are inadequate in others.

Diagnosing personalities is a complex business, and will always be beset by qualifications about the interaction of persons and environments, as is this example of serving officers. It is more useful to look at dynamic factors – the interplay of motives and the means to fulfil them, of ambitions and human objectives. For example, it is not true to say that there are two distinct personality types, the moderate drinker and the alcoholic, for one often becomes the other at a period of financial stress. It is better to ask what people are doing, and why they are doing it, at the time when they first develop the signs of distorted dependence.

[3] 1 Corinthians 3:16, 17; 6:19, 20; Romans 12:1-12; Ephesians 2:1-10.

[4] R. Cockett, *Drug Abuse and Personality in Young Offenders* (Butterworth, 1971).

WHY DO THEY DO IT?

When the victims of distorted dependence are asked why they do what they do, there are recurring themes in their replies. Unhappily, I cannot claim to have studied this scientifically, since I have never conducted an unbiased survey. It could and should be done. But it has been my experience in many interviews with alcoholics, over-eaters and drug-dependent people that certain objectives are shared. This view in fact has been confirmed, with ample references to records, by Nicholi.[5] Open as this is to the criticism of hearing what one wants to hear, it is also an open invitation to the properly critical reader to check the ideas by listening for himself. This paper stands or falls upon that. It does not come easily to a clinical scientist to write about what is really a clinical impression, based upon a number of anecdotal cases. I am well aware, however, of these shortcomings, as I am of the difficulty of gaining reliable scientific evidence in the whole field of psychiatry, and also of the pressing urgency of the problems. In psychiatry, after all, science in its conventional form (by that I mean the physical sciences) is beyond access, since every observation must be interpreted through at least *two* minds, and independent validation is seldom possible.

Is it possible to analyse the patients' objectives? Four seem especially prominent.

a. A search for a 'prop' upon which to depend

At first sight this seems silly. Are not these people already thoroughly dependent when they come for help? How can they be said to be searching for dependence? More careful enquiry, however, shows that this impression is too superficial. Their searching

[5] Armand Nicholi, work presented to the Fourth International Congress of Christian Physicians, Toronto, on 19 July 1972.

for satisfaction is confessed by the more articulate patients. It may begin with sniffing petrol fumes, glue solvents or tobacco. They may then try alcohol, barbiturates or cannabis. Then they will try heroin. They stop there only because it is the strongest thing they can find. Some compulsive alcoholics will search for stronger solace in boot or metal polish, methylated spirits, or eau-de-Cologne. If these people cannot obtain the strongest, they will take a weaker drug for a time.

They often transfer from one drug to another. Many patients have made this clear; their dependence is less specific than might appear. Something went wrong in their motivation *before* they started obtaining their favourite drug, and remains abnormal when they cannot obtain it. In a small survey made by the author some years ago amongst overweight diabetic women, it was found that those who could lose weight by dieting were significantly more often those who transferred to alcohol or tobacco, whilst those who could not lose weight tended to avoid these things.[6]

[6] The patients were grouped by rigorous prior criteria into those who succeeded in losing weight by dieting (**S**), those who failed (**F**) and those who succeeded initially, but later failed (**ISF**). The frequencies of tobacco and alcohol consumption in these groups were

	S (10)	**F (4)**	**ISF (9)**
Tobacco	5	1	2
Alcohol	4	1	2 (both only very occasionally)
Neither tobacco nor alcohol taken	3	3	7

If these are more simply grouped we have the following :

	Long-term success	**Long-term failure**
Regular tobacco or alcohol taken	9	4
Neither drug taken regularly	3	12

The effect is significant at the 0.05 level.

So the same phenomena occur in relation to food as well as to drugs. There is even a food equivalent of compulsive alcoholism. A woman whose parents perished in one of Hitler's concentration camps weighed 185 kgm. (about 29 stone), though she ate fairly normally by day. Only patient and persistent history-taking revealed that, when nightmares woke her, as often happened, she would come down to seek solace in the larder, sometimes eating a whole loaf at one sitting.

Once this picture has been seen and understood, it seems very odd that most people believe that the centre of the 'drug problem' is the drug! More often it is the drug taker who is most of the problem, and was so before he ever took the drug. It is true that some drugs are strongly addictive. But it is also true that most of those who are now hooked on them were deliberately seeking this. It is interesting to note that opiates taken for severe pain seldom lead to dependence or to pleasure in those who need them. Yet, as a rule, opiates taken for their other actions evoke dependence. Clearly it is not the drug alone that is to blame.

It has also been pointed out that one property which drugs of dependence have in common, whether they give pleasure or blot out unpleasant feelings, is that satisfaction comes first, and the 'pay-off' much later. For example, food satisfies the emotions immediately; the over-eater suffers the miseries of gross obesity only later. The same goes for alcohol and heroin. There is more to drug dependence, however, than this simple psychological truism, as will soon be shown. There is a major spiritual component too.

b. A desire to modify the mind

This may be to avoid misery, or to gain a transcendental experience or 'high'. The alcoholic often speaks of 'blotting it out', the heroin addict of 'losing his pain'.

For others it may merely be escape from the boredom of their motiveless living.[7] Many young people are bitterly critical of their parents for failure to show them a meaning in life and their intense emotion is so painful that they wish to suppress or change it. It is escape from and escape into: from pain and into a withdrawn, dreamy, untroubled state. For the more intellectual there is the added notion of expanded experience, broadened musical performance or perceptive painting.

The fascinating fact is that the effect obtained depends upon what the devotee expects, and the social milieu to which he belongs. Just as the experience of eating a first-class dinner seems to vary, depending upon where and with whom it is eaten, so the effects of most drugs depend upon the social and psychological surroundings. It is interesting that some drugs taken to modify the mind induce or cement dependence (heroin, alcohol, barbiturates), whilst others do not seem to do so (lysergide) or do so only transitorily (cannabis), even though the dependence may last for a long time. So this desire to modify the mind is not necessarily a characteristic of dependence, though commonly linked with it. But the dependent person always craves a solace of some kind, which must in and of itself involve a desire to modify awareness.

c. A desire to compensate for real or imagined rejection

The 'pain' which the victim of distorted dependence feels, and for which he seeks solace, is often a feeling of rejection : a feeling which need not represent the true state of affairs. Patients have described their homes as places where they felt rejected, humiliated or criticized by parents when their brothers and sisters were not.

[7] A. Nicholi, *op. cit.*

Kurt Hahn wrote to *The Times* about a boy who felt rejected because he was not picked for a team to which it had long been his ambition to belong. A young heroin-dependent girl told the author how she left home when she realized for the first time that her highly respectable mother did not really care for her at all, a flash of insight which came in one very brief conversation. Many drug dependents in Whitechapel come from a group who feel rejected by the 'upper classes'. This they not unreasonably infer from the dreary, insanitary and squalid rows in which they seem confined without escape. Often the anger which is felt is turned inwards and self-inflicted, in a kind of self-rejection.[8]

d. A desire to 'resocialize', to identify with a group

This is the obverse of (**c**). Drug dependents describe it as a chief reason for choosing drugs, and use almost religious jargon to describe it. They want to belong to a group with a common language, a common quest, and a common interest and method. They want to share in a mystery. They may recruit others, and in doing so may demonstrate a kind of evangelistic zeal. Again, this is not the *sine qua non* of distorted dependence – there are solitary alcoholics, for example. Most over-eaters are solitary. But it is a very common feature with cannabis, heroin, and even with LSD. It may be partly for this reason that rehabilitation of heroin dependents, always a difficult thing after drug withdrawal, depends greatly upon the social milieu. A supportive *group* is an almost indispensable tool for achieving success. It may not be a matter of actual rejection, but rather a feeling of profound alienation from adults which makes young people respond to pressures from their peers,[9] pressures

[8] A. Nicholi, *op. cit.*
[9] A. Nicholi, *op. cit.*

which come to demand a response as pitilessly as the adult authoritarianism from which they have sought to escape.

DIAGNOSIS

Psychiatry has failed so far to isolate the typical personality of a dependent – if it exists. There is no more than a hint as to how the disorder is caused. And psychiatric treatment yields very poor results. Nevertheless, the psychiatric contribution on this account should not be despised or disregarded. It is extremely useful in dealing with many aspects of the problem. But psychiatrists have not yet attained a *radical* understanding of dependence. It doesn't help much to be told that you are inadequate (it was a recognition of this fact that made many sufferers search for a prop anyway). Nor does it promise well for effective therapy. The results of conventional medical treatment are also notoriously poor in this area, though real but sparse successes are obtained where a major amount of group support can be found, as for example with Alcoholics Anonymous, or Weight Watchers. So where can people go for more help?

Here there comes an important question. Is distorted dependence *only* a weakness, a minor mental or physical illness or abnormality? Is it a tendency that people are born with, or catch, or a degeneration which attacks their bodily or mental functions? Or is there a spiritual, or motivational, problem here? Many sufferers seem to have lost their will-power, whether the problem is how to diet, or how to get off drugs or the bottle. Can an analysis of the problem in the spiritual dimension help? Certainly it should not oust worth-while psychiatric or physical remedies any more than they should aim to exclude a spiritual approach. The true diagnosis involves the whole person, in all his aspects, and much harm has been done by pressing spiritual ideas in opposition to psychiatry, and psychiatry in opposition to a spiritual approach.

To those who find the word 'spiritual' odd or without content, or synonymous with 'mind', some definition is owed. There is an area within a man's person, or an aspect of it, which is supreme. It is that aspect concerned with will, with choice, with motives. The central 'I' which decides, wants, needs and feels. It is not that aspect which by adding twos makes fours, nor that which instinctively may prefer mauve hats to green, or blondes to brunettes. It is an aspect which notes, compares and then co-ordinates choice. It is the part which feels 'I must', or 'I ought', or 'that is wrong', or 'that is right', a part which can become aware of God. Here the word 'part' is not used to imply some anatomically distinct 'lump' within the mind, some area of brain. It is, as was said, an aspect, or projection, of the whole person.

Now no-one can prove scientifically that such a thing exists; no-one can get his scientific 'hands' on the problem. But we know such things by introspection, and by sharing the results with others who also introspect. We also know them by revelation, that is, because they have been described for us in the Bible in passages which claim to be 'God-breathed' or inspired. What we read there corresponds to the realities of behaviour which we see in ourselves and in others. So there is what philosophers might call 'ontological' evidence for the existence of a spiritual dimension in man, and distorted dependence is supremely a disorder of this aspect of man's life. It is above all present when people are trapped in a system of false choices, almost in spite of themselves.

If you have met and talked with such folk, you must have felt that they are like a watch with a broken main spring. It can be wound a little, and ticks for a few seconds, but soon stops again. They seem to have a snapped choice mechanism. Again and again they rise from their habit only to fall weakly once more. Knowing that their choices are false and will damage them, they nevertheless relentlessly and helplessly do what they know must hurt them and make what they know to be inferior choices. That is a spiritual problem, at least in part, and is susceptible to spiritual analysis in ways which could never be true of, say, a broken leg or a cold in the head.

A SPIRITUAL ANALYSIS

If we want a spiritual analysis then, surely, the Bible is the obvious place to look for it. If distorted dependence really has a spiritual component we should expect to find it discussed there. In the next few pages, therefore, the reader is asked to do some homework! I have listed four passages from the New Testament and suggest that these should be read and studied for the light they throw on the problem we are discussing, before moving on to the sections that follow. This, no doubt, will be a test of our motivation. But it is more than that. The Bible must be allowed to act by itself as the vehicle for spiritual ideas. Apart from a brief explanation of the context of each passage, therefore, no attempt is made to provide a commentary. Instead, there are a number of questions on each passage, followed by a summary of my own understanding of its relevance to our subject. This the reader is invited to compare with his own conclusions.

The first passage: John 6: 1-71

BACKGROUND

A large crowd had followed Jesus to hear his message. They needed food and were far from home. No-one had come prepared for several days' outdoor life. Also, they were stirred by nationalism, and looking for a king.

QUESTIONS

1. What did the people want (verses 2, 26)?

2. Did Jesus think that they did not need what they wanted (verse 5)?

3. Did Jesus agree with their beliefs about their own needs (verse 27)? Why did he withdraw from them twice (verses 3, 15, 22)?

4. If what they wanted was needful to them, and they were prepared to follow Christ so far, why were they wrong to seek it as they did (verses 14, 15, 24)?

5. What was the nature of their error? Was it progressive? *Cf.* verses 2 and 26, then study verses 28, 30, 34. See verses 27, 29, 32 and 35 as replies to verses 26, 28, 30 and 34 respectively.

6. What does verse 36 mean? See Jesus' radical critique of their view in verses 63 and 64.

7. Was the mistake confined to the multitude, or did Jesus' disciples also misunderstand (verses 6, 7, 9, 66, 71)?

8. Why did Jesus link 'bread' with his 'flesh' (verses 41 - 59)?

9. Is independence possible (verses 7, 28, 53, 66-69)?

10. If anyone could have afforded to be independent, it was Jesus, the perfect man, the Author of all that exists. Was he independent (verses 11, 27, 29, 32, 37-40, 44, 57, 65)? If Jesus found it impossible, will it not also be so for us, since the lesser is included in the greater?

11. Is there, then, a true, desirable state of dependence?

12. Are there lesser things on which we may come to depend, which substitute for greater satisfactions? Can one dependence be substituted for another (*cf.* Ephesians 5: 18)?

SUMMARY

From what you have read and thought, do you feel able to agree with this summary, or does it fail to represent the sense of John 6?

1. People need, and depend upon, bread, which is very satisfying.

2. God recognizes this, and provides bread.

3. False attitudes arise in two ways: first, a desire to become independent of God; second, a desire to become content with the gift whilst ignoring the Giver.

4. When a lesser good satisfies, it becomes a 'prop', a focus for distorted dependence. It then obscures the greater good, which in fact would have contained the lesser, satisfying all aspects of the person fully and redeeming him.

5. Distorted dependence, and reliance upon props, can occur amongst Christians as well as others. God is not content to allow anyone to rest satisfied with false solutions to their problems. A partial solution of man's problems prevents the radical solution from taking place. The good becomes the enemy of the best. A man's body needs bread; the whole man needs Christ and bread.

The second passage: 2 Corinthians 12: 1-12

BACKGROUND

In this passage Paul replies to some at Corinth who were critical of his efforts on their behalf, dubious of his apostolic status, and boastful of their own ability to see spiritual visions. Paul probably had a weak personal appearance which gave them added reason for their contemptuous dismissal of him. This may have been increased by an eye complaint, perhaps the 'thorn in the flesh' referred to in verse 7.

QUESTIONS

1. Was Paul a true apostle (verses 11, 12)?
2. Did Paul also have transcendental experiences (verses 1-4, 6)?
3. Did he rely on them as an important escape from pain, or escape into spirituality (verses 5-7)?
4. Did God relieve Paul's sufferings through transcendental experience (verses 8-10)?
5. Was there a good higher than escape (verses 9-10)?

SUMMARY

From what you have read and thought, do you think what follows to be a fair summary of the passage, or do you not?

1. God allows and gives transcendental experiences, but they are better engendered by him than induced by drugs or alcohol (*cf.* Ephesians 5:18).
2. These experiences are not given to permit escape from pain or to justify religious acceptance by others.
3. Reliance upon God's grace transcends experiences, and is the answer to mental pain.
4. This is no surprise, since in a sense the message is identical with John chapter 6. 'Experiences', like 'bread', can become a prop. God wants us, rather, to relate to him *and* enjoy experiences.
5. Experiences again can become a route to independence. God desires us instead to rely continually upon his grace.

The third passage: 1 Peter 2: 1-25

BACKGROUND

Peter was immensely impressed by the sufferings of Christ, which at first left him puzzled, frightened and dismayed. But after Pentecost they became a source of immense strength to him and something he became willing to share in some measure. Those sufferings, and the way in which they were borne, had the stamp of deity, of a source of life which obviously transcended the merely human and temporal.

QUESTIONS

1. Is human rejection something which happens in isolation, or is there another, Godward, side to the problem (verses 4-10)?
2. Does human rejection mark the end of achievement, and does it render a situation hopeless (verses 21-25)?
3. Reception into human circles is something for which men long naturally. Is it the most desirable end of life? See the whole passage but especially verses 9, 10, 19, 20, 25.
4. If human *rejection* does not rule out *reception* by God, should that reception become an end in itself (verse 9)?
5. What is the purpose of reception amongst God's people, whether or not human rejection goes with it (verses 5, 9, 12)?
6. Should those who feel rejected by men return a like rejection of human authority (verses 11-14, 17, 18, 23)?
7. Can a Christian expect to avoid suffering (verse 21)?
8. What, in fact, is his calling, the fulfilment of which brings divine approval (verses 20-21)?
9. Is this fair? Does God ask us to bear a rejection which he has not suffered himself (verses 21, 23, 24)?
10. How may our 'wounds' be healed (verses 24, 25)?
11. Compare verses 9 and 7. Can reception into God's race, priesthood, nation or people become a 'prop' which provides satisfaction but prevents a more vital fellowship with him?
12. What is the true meening of freedom (verses 16 and context, 24, 25)?

SUMMARY

Is it accurate to say that for those who 'suffer rejection' these verses afford a radical explanation of their situation, put another side to the argument, and show that neither reception nor rejection is the major aspect of their problem? A more vital objective than reception amongst men is to learn personal communion with God, the meaning of suffering, and the meaning of freedom. True freedom is not found in rebellion, but in submission to the truth as it really is. One cannot gain fellowship with God by 'knocking' what he has ordained.

The fourth passage: Philippians 3: 1-21

BACKGROUND

Groups of Christians with a strong Jewish affiliation were trying to enforce circumcision upon the early church as a means to gain or retain self-respect, and identity with their own religious forbears. Paul, realizing that this was no necessary part of Christianity, and that the motives from which it sprang were disreputable, censured the movement strongly (verses 2, 3).

QUESTIONS

1. Is there an example here of people who are prepared to suffer and damage themselves to satisfy the intense desire to conform and to identify with a group (verse 2)?
2. What word does Paul use to express the focus of their confidence and reliance (verse 3)?
3. What does the term 'flesh' mean in Paul's writings? Does it refer only to acts done by the physical body (verses 4, 5, 19)?
4. Does identification with one group as an act of 'the flesh' lead to enmity against other groups (verse 6)?
5. Does this happen only when the chosen identity involves something that is wrong? Can it happen even when it is in principle a good identification (verse 6)?
6. Who is the only worthy focus for identification and imitation (verses 7-11)?

7. Can a *good* focus then become the enemy of the *best*? Contrast verse 6 and verse 9.
8. What is the highest form of identification (verses 8-10)?
9. What does 'knowing him' mean here? Is it a nodding acquaintance, or a deeply meaningful working relationship?
10. Do the errors of past affiliations set a permanent block in the way of developing better relationships (verses 13, 14)?
11. What is a Christian's true, mature 'group affiliation' and why does this make a strong desire for lesser relationships illogical (verses 15, 16, 20, 21)?
12. Are 'peer group' drives a good thing in principle, or should one always aim to be independent (verse 17)?
13. What is the ultimate fate of the Christian's body, which is the spring and source of the 'desires of the flesh' (verse 21)?

SUMMARY

Is it, or is it not, the sense of this passage that 'props', those entities which are less than the best but which can become so wholly satisfying, are shown to have their source in 'the flesh', the area of selfish instinctive desires and drives? Is it not also true that God does not expect people to deny the instincts he has given but rather invites them to work them out in the context of fellowship with him? This is logical only when one escapes from bondage to time, and sees life in the light of eternity, when the physical body will cease to be in its present form but God will persist as the means of life and satisfaction. This is not living only for eternity, but rather living in time, *really* living in time, in the light of eternity.

SO WHAT DO WE DO NOW?

a. A spiritual 'diagnosis'

It has surely been established that there are areas within the Bible which are immensely relevant to the problem of distorted dependence, areas which have a surprising commentary upon it, which provide a profound analysis of it. If you like they provide a spiritual diagnosis, or 'understanding-through' of it. They are often quoted for entirely different reasons. Indeed, I was unaware of their relevance to this problem until I re-read them in this context. These passages are by no means the only ones to provide insights into the problem; there are many more, because the Bible develops a spiritual diagnosis of human problems out of human history. Because there is this relevant information, and because the Bible is intended to be a very practical book, it clearly follows that any attempt to help the victims of distorted dependence will be incomplete without its insights. Naturally enough, those who are victims are often unwilling to accept a biblical analysis of this problem, but that is not a reason for withholding it from them.

There seems to be a striking contrast here between the methods of the biblical writers on the one hand and many modern psychotherapists on the other. While the latter often aim only to help a man to understand his situation as it is and for himself, by helping him to ask and answer the right questions about it, the Bible strikes home by declaring an analysis of the problem from a source outside man, which reveals a diagnosis to him - a process which can hurt before it heals and which will often be unacceptable to the sufferer. It also shows him not only who he is but who he could become. It refuses to accept 'is' as 'ought to be'. It goes further. Psychotherapy and counselling involve recognition of realities but then often seem to leave the sufferer to 'pull himself up by his own shoe-laces'. It is no surprise, therefore, that relapse is common. God offers 'grace', however, a word which implies no mere analysis and encouragement, but *enabling*. It is so important to know what that word 'grace' means in 2 Corinthians 12.

The problem, then, is how, practically, to bring help where it is needed.

b. Difficulties of communicating the diagnosis

If a Christian wants to help someone who is drug-dependent, his first ambition must surely be to rid himself of those prejudices and hypocrisies which are so common, but which are no part of true Christianity. Why, for example, that exclusive paranoid focusing upon 'drugs' as 'the cause' of the problem, when it clearly has a far wider setting within human personality? And why the condemnation of 'wrong' substrates for distorted dependence (drugs, too much alcohol) when those which are 'right' (religious observance, sectarianism, food, the 'right' amount of alcohol) pass unnoticed? The sickening tragedy of Northern Ireland surely shows how dependence upon religious and national affiliations ('good' objectives) can coexist with extreme violence and evil in many hearts. Though it is impossible to be quantitative about this, and though examples of distorted dependence seem less frequent within than without the professing church, they are still so easy to find within it that they must be a serious barrier to faith among those who are not committed to a church.

Remember that the disciples got Christ's message wrong nearly as much as did the crowd. A testimony to the saving power of Christ will not seem very real to non-Christians if they can see many victims of distorted dependence within the church. And we must not forget that religious observance is probably the commonest 'prop' of the lot. It is to be sharply distinguished from faith. Religion is what I do for God. Faith is reliance upon what God has done, and will do, for me. The people in John chapter 6 asked how they might do the works of God, in order to make bread and become independent of him. Jesus withdrew from them. It is only when the church learns the meaning of distorted dependence, both within and without itself that it will become able to help those who suffer from it.

A Christian's second ambition should be to bear witness to what he knows and understands. But such an understanding cannot be enforced or enjoined (any more than Paul's Pharisaism could be enjoined in Philippians 3). To try to enforce Christian belief would be a direct example of 'the flesh'. Unfortunately some Christians' enthusiasm has at times surpassed their devotion to biblical truth, an understandable but unhappy thing. But every Christian should know that he has a logical, relevant and coherent case to present.

The next problem is how to present so subtle a case. This booklet will speak only to those who are trying to help dependent folk in an informed way, or to those dependent people who are among the more perceptive and thoughtful. It will scarcely help the drug-dependent folk I have met in Whitechapel. But can the sophisticated insights of faith be presented to those whose very problem shows their lack of appreciation of them? This should not daunt the thoughtful Christian too much, though it should make him think very carefully, because Jesus Christ, and Paul, had just this very task of presenting new and involved ideas to darkened minds. And they succeeded. After all, there were Corinthian and Philippian Christians to be written to, and there is still a church today. Some have been able to understand! How did they do it? Jesus had the overwhelming advantage of his signs. Because he multiplied bread, because he taught with authority and not like the scribes, people were drawn to him, felt obliged to listen and carefully considered even his most obscure statements. Even his enemies felt obliged to learn and analyse all he said, in an effort to denigrate him. This raises the next vital point.

People will heed only a message that works in practice. Does the Christian message help those who suffer from distorted dependence?

It must be said that if there is anything that *does* help it will be obvious immediately. The results of medical and psychiatric efforts have been very poor. The numbers who gained relief from them for over five years seldom exceeded 15% in a carefully worked-up series of cases. The 'props' in these cases were drugs, alcohol, tobacco and food. Usually it is much less than 15%. And notice that these belong to a series of selected, favourable cases, selected because they have 'asked' for relief. Social rehabilitation may have been more successful, but accurate figures are lacking. If someone leaves the associations which evoke dependence and is helped to build a new life with new friends, success is more likely. Against that rather desolate background any effective remedy will show up brightly. How, then, does a true Christian faith compare?

The answer is that so few try it that there are not enough cases to compare. After all, only about 4% of the community are regularly practising Christians. But where it *has* been embraced this faith has liberated men and women. I well remember a notorious drunkard in the town where my grandmother lived. This man's family were neglected and he could not work normally. He became a Christian, and his life was lastingly transformed, to the delight of many in the district. That sort of thing cannot be forgotten. In more recent years other patients have been seen to be similarly released. It is no light thing when a man, referred for care to a well-known Anglican treatment centre for alcoholics, returns two years later, to tell you that for the first time in his married life he has been able to afford a car and take his wife and children on holiday. That man had no doubt that it was not just the tablets and the rehabilitation, but his new-found Saviour who had released him. There have even been within my own knowledge three or four who have been able to give up heroin.

Is it only a Christian faith which can do this? No, it is not. A successful marriage and the coming of a child did it for another young man after two medical attempts at heroin withdrawal had failed. He even returned later to repay from his new earnings the money that the social workers had lent him - a real test of cure! Marriage is a strong force in anyone's emotional life. Obviously marriage is a very hazardous thing in a background of drug dependence, and usually it leads only to worse tragedies. But in this case it was the right way out.

It is no surprise that these things happen. Do not forget that dependence props are interchangeable. Patients can convert from food to tobacco and back again and regularly switch from one drug to another. The principle is simply that any source of satisfaction which is of sufficient emotional strength can displace any other. Why then the emphasis on Christian faith? Simply because the passages which we have studied above show that a proper relationship to God, and the fullness of satisfaction which can be found in him, are logically the strongest and most complete supports of them all and are what God wishes us to enjoy. Can these be prescribed medically? Of course not. They are only for 'as many as received him'. But this fact gives no excuse for offering only the good instead of the best.

c. Insight from understanding

How should this message be offered? This is the central problem. It is no use rushing in with the brash message 'You need Christ', any more than it helps other sick people to say 'Medicine is the answer', with no more explanation than that. Who is Christ? Where is he now? How can he possibly help me? These are the inevitable questions, whether they are spoken or silent. There is also no point in offering Christ *instead* of medical and social help. Christ himself offered the knowledge of God *and bread* to the people. 'Your heavenly Father knoweth that ye have need of all these things. But seek ye first the kingdom of God, and his righteousness; and all these things shall be added unto you' (Matthew 6: 32, 33, AV). God offers himself, and 'things' too. We need both. But we should seek him first. We bear witness, therefore, that the displacing power of a new affection can enable people to handle the 'things' of life without their becoming 'props' of distorted dependence.

A CHECK LIST OF SUGGESTED 'DO'S' AND 'DON'TS'

This list is given not to make it unnecessary to read what has gone before, but to crystallize the application of ideas to the practical problem, and for the reader to check his understanding of the argument for himself.

1. Try to learn about distorted dependence before setting out to help, so that misunderstandings will not be propagated.

2. Don't focus solely on the 'prop' or drug, but remember the sufferer's emotional problems.

3. Don't imagine that it is *either* medicine, psychiatry *or* spiritual help that is needed. It is all three. And equally important is the social support of loving, caring surroundings for as long as they are needed.

4. Try not to force help prematurely on those who do

not want it. Some are keen to admit they are sick, and also keen to stay sick! Do try to identify those whose appeal for help is real but disguised. It could even be a suicidal attempt, for example. If that evokes contempt or alienation in your heart, do not try to help someone until you have learnt better.

5. Don't think that a Christian analysis of these problems is easy to understand or communicate. Do try to study the most helpful ways to get the insights across.

6. Don't imagine that, when someone sees his problem for what it really is, he will necessarily feel helped, relieved or grateful. Do try always to point to the way of escape alongside the hurtful insights. Remember that Christ invites people to a way which he has travelled himself, at the same time providing his grace which is sufficient.

7. Don't force knowledge too rapidly. It is better patiently to educate than to build false confidence on slick 'answers'. Always remember that the power of Christ in someone's life is equal to their deepest need if they are really willing to let him deal with it. Remember they may want to hurry, to rely on themselves, to be independent. Christ specifically abrogated each of these ideas in John chapter 6.

8. Don't try to help sufferers from distorted dependence prematurely if this is your own major weakness. Try to apply the principles at home before they are offered outside. Though weakness brings a special understanding, it remains a focus of temptation too.

9. Remember the weakness and the wounds of sufferers from dependence. Even when they have been released from their dependence. it is usually unwise for them ever to return to a former drug. Full abstinence is usually their wisest course. A proper belief in the power of Christ should not make us overlook their individual weakness. Temptation is a real danger, and all the worse if it comes unwittingly from helpers who happen to be stronger and able to avoid dependence.

10. Don't think that all that is needed is talk. The facts of faith are often better caught than taught. They often come to people slowly after watching many hours of Christian living in a friend. In this kind of situation the 'caring community' is the best preacher. Don't forget that the wounds were caused by years of evil within and without a person, often beginning in infancy or in the teenage years. They were learnt from acts, and often can be healed only through acts.

11. Don't imagine that anything less than the knowledge of God in Christ, and of the whole of life seen in that context, will suffice a needy person. They should not imagine that they are different from others in this respect, or worse off. To transfer from distorted dependence upon food or drugs to that upon religion would be disastrous. Jesus wished people to become satisfied in *him.* So the positive aim must be this, not merely cure, or happiness, or better experiences, or better friends, or solace in rejection, or transfer of dependence. Nor should it be the *emotional investment of would-be helpers* in the problem! Christians must search their emotions to be certain that they are not just trying to gain satisfaction, or trying to relieve their own emotional tensions, by inflicting a false help on others. That is not loving, even to oneself.

Last of all, an important warning is needed. The ideas expressed here are based partly on known research, partly on individuals' experience, partly on theory and partly on the Bible. The truth of it all will be seen only when it can be further tested experimentally. No-one should fall into the rationalistic fallacy of accepting it as an appealing argument. We must be thorough empiricists. This is written in the hope that more people will try it out, and see if it works.